Murmurations

Murmurations

Poems by Art Nahill

First published 2017 by Two Hemispheres Poetry
9 Towle Place, Auckland 1050
New Zealand

Copyright © Art Nahill 2017

The right of Art Nahill to be identified
as the author of this work in terms of section 96 of the Copyright Act 1994 is
hereby asserted.

All rights reserved. Apart from any fair dealing for the purposes of private
study, research, criticism or review, as permitted under copyright law, no part
may be reproduced by any process without the permission of the publisher.

Produced by Mary Egan Publishing, www.maryegan.co.nz
Printed in New Zealand

ISBN 978-0-473-43053-5
ISBN (Epub) 978-0-473-43054-2

Contents

I

Echolocation	8
Multitudes	9
The Rooms We Leave	10
Athazagoraphobia	11
Magician Dreams	12
Long Night Moon	13
Achluophobia	14
Housefly	15
Inchoate	16
Memory as Diagnosis	17
Heroes	18
Superstitions	19
A Brief History of Salt	20
Chronometrophobia	22
Claustrophobia	23

II

Hometown	26
Good Friday	28
The Great Molasses Flood Boston, 1919	29
On Edward Hopper's *Rooms by the Sea*, 1951	30
Malaprops	31
The Parrot	32
Breen's Funeral Parlor	33
Ritual	34
Vandals	35
Mr. Dombrinski	36
Fieldstone Wall	37

Commitment	38
One Hundred and Two	39
Murmurations	40
Kingfisher	41
The Evolution of Wings	42
Ennui	43

III

To My Cat Asleep Across the Keyboard	46
Ars Poetica #37	47
Ars Poetica #78	48
You Say My Poems Have Too Many Adjectives	49
Crosswords	50
Synesthesia	51
Ode to a Platypus	52
Man Has Arm Reattached After Shark Attack	53
Our War Correspondent Files This Report from Dusk	54
Survival Guide	55
Man Crushed by 6000 Pound Boulder in Own Backyard	56
Nocturne #47	57
Ophidiophobia	58
Arachnophobia	59
Walking the Dog	60
Damn Right I Let the Cat Out	61
Turbulence	62
Benedictions	63
The Day the Music Died	64
Black Swans	65
The Green and Golden Bell Frog	66
Guilty	67
Acknowledgements	68

I

O the night is coming on
And I am nobody's son
— STANLEY KUNITZ

Echolocation

I navigate between
sky and stone

stone and the reflection
of stone. The trees sing

back to me in my own
voice. I have no need

for vision my ears fine-tuned
to the night's faint frequencies

hunting echoes
making my way through the dark

by steering
toward the silences.

Multitudes

I carry many deaths
inside me though
not as a cat is said to

or a saint bristling
with arrows.
Not as an oak

in winter flies
its few brown flags
of surrender.

Not the way the womb
sheds its lush red lining.
Not the way a virus storms

the cockpit of a cell
but the way a man
feeding pigeons in the park

watches each evening
as they wander off
when his hands are empty.

The Rooms We Leave

Doors slam
decisively in our wake

sofas and chairs
unimpressed

by what we took
ourselves to be.

Mirrors mock
the hats we wore

our frequent
furtive glances.

The silence sings
its single perfect note

uninterrupted
by the staccato

of casual conversation.
The tabletop basks

uncluttered
in the sun. The air

stretches out
filling in

our absence
breathlessly.

Athazagoraphobia

Every day I check the mail
sometimes twice for evidence
of my existence, hope

that the blinking button
of the answering machine
can prove conclusively
I've not been erased

even if it's a wrong number
someone inquiring about the cost
of kitchen renovation.

Every morning I recite
my name aloud before the mirror
affix it firmly to my face
reapply it every few hours
like cheap makeup.

What I need is a mnemonic
to remember myself by
to become a catchy melody
I can't get out of my head.

But I find myself losing
bits of me
day after leprous day

until I fear I'll wake
to find one morning I've made
not the slightest of impressions
upon the sheets.

Magician Dreams

I slip into the black
tuxedo of sleep
unshackle myself

above a giant tank
of piranha
        catch
the bullet
between my teeth
blindfolded
at fifty paces.

My lovely assistant
saws me into halves
the faith of the audience
in illusion
growing more
unshakeable

with each pull
of her bare and slender arms.

For my finale
I will levitate
hover momentarily
like an angel
then vanish
into the nothingness
up my sleeves.

Long Night Moon

—full moon closest to the winter solstice

Beneath this
naked bulb

only facts
and denials:

my name
in the old country

means *one*
who endures.

I do not believe
the world speaks

to me in omens—
though in the pressing

dark my bogeymen
crouch, keen as hounds.

If they catch me
Orion warns

my life will be briefer
than tomorrow.

Achluophobia

We speak of darkness
as though it were

the quiet neighbor
no one suspected

the bag left unattended
in a crowded station.

We speak of darkness
as though it were merely

absence   a lack
like love or money

a kind of trade
wind bearing hungry ships

to new continents
though darkness

is indigenous to this place

the reason we hesitate
at the top of the stairs

sleep
with the hall light on.

Does anyone choose
his ghosts?

Tonight clouds
mask what light

the moon can muster.

No one chooses.

It's a lifetime
until morning.

Housefly

The weak winter sun
puddling at the windows
has been enough
to resurrect it

like a rogue memory
of you
      careening

into   things
slamming against
    the glass

a punch-drunk fighter
who doesn't know enough
to stay down

though being cold-blooded
it will soon fall back

to the dusty sill
or behind the couch

with daylight rushing on
as it does
this time of year.

Inchoate

From my window
I watch the park

slowly filling
after days of rain

the way I'd walk
up and down

past your house
even in the pouring rain

as though I had somewhere
to go

when I was fourteen
and slowly filling

filling

but without
the words

to say
with what.

Memory as Diagnosis

My mother
in the blue

TV light 1979
the sound of the evening

news turned
all the way down.

I'm waiting
for my father again

the sky jaundiced
above the city

the homebound
traffic passing

a faint murmur
in the failing heart

of America.

Heroes

He kissed you
on Christmas and anniversaries.
You slept in separate beds

in a room without doors.
He left you
every morning for good

returning every evening
for supper and the sake
of the kids. We didn't understand

loneliness then
why you kept
a leather belt handy

in the kitchen drawer
to spread across our skin
like salve

when we toppled knick-knacks
or made too much noise
as our TV heroes:

Hercules
Thor
Guardians of the Universe.

Afterward you'd lie
curtains drawn
the room dark

except for the pulsing
orange flare of your cigarette.
We didn't know

how to rescue you
and so would grow
quietly mortal.

Superstitions

After the divorce
you moved us to the city

where the nights were not so full
of owls. You read your horoscope

religiously each morning
kept a garland of dried garlic

by the door. Our new house
had no mirrors.

Every Friday the Thirteenth
you spent in bed

curtains drawn.
Triskaidekaphobia

that's what it's called
in the lexicon of fears.

Why some hotels skip
the thirteenth floor

and airplanes
the thirteenth row

the number cursed
by the thirteen

who took part
in the Last Supper

and Judas Iscariot
the thirteenth to arrive.

That's how you explained it—
you who'd been betrayed

by so many
kisses.

A Brief History of Salt

To say *salt*

is to invoke
antiquity

salary

the salt wages
paid to Roman soldiers.

Say *salt*

preservative
purifier

sealer of covenants.

Pharaohs
Buddhist monks
mummified with it.

Gandhi marching
to the sea for it.

Say *salt*

mined
or brine-sprung

the residuum
of evaporation.

You
demanded a pinch

over our right shoulder
when we spilled the shaker

threw a handful
on Father's coffin

to ward off
evil.

Look back
and be turned

into a pillar
of it.

What gives taste
to tears

burns
in the open wound.

Chronometrophobia

Think   think

insists the unblinking

face looming
like a schoolteacher's—

severe in its disapproval
this sleepless hour

a dry wind flustering
the trees outside.

Think   think
the voice

sharp
        metallic

hands outstretched
pitiless

as those of the strangers my parents
warned me of as a child.

Claustrophobia

During the commercials
my brother
would pin me to the carpet
Killer Kowalski style
until I cried
or *Saturday Morning Wrestling*
came back on.

⋆

My grandfather told me
of a miner friend
trapped for days
in a space not big enough
to sit up in
pissing and shitting himself
until they finally winched
him out.

⋆

My father so wracked
by cancer
was waked in a closed casket.
We threw fistfuls of dirt
on top of him
while the bulldozer
idled
in the shade.

II

You're just a citizen
of your own familiarity
who can't remember himself in a different way

— TONY HOAGLAND

Hometown

Nineteen twelve
the National Guard
called in to break the Bread
and Roses strike.

That made the newsreels
even in Europe.

Frost published
his first poems
in the local paper.

Leonard Bernstein
was born here

and Robert Goulet
who crooned
from hi-fi's
Friday nights

aunts and uncles over
for drinks and dinner.

For a time
in the Guinness
Book of Records
home to the largest textile mill
under one roof

though the place went bust
after the war
when cloth
then shoes
then most everything else
came cheaper
from overseas.

Still,
its streets and stores
were familiar.

In seventh-grade
I sat behind Lisa O'Donnell

in Father Flynn's
geography class

her Midwestern-colored hair
the long coastlines of her legs.

The park was flooded
every winter
into a skating rink

and snow days off
from school
we sledded down
Reservoir Hill

that long white
sheet of possibility.

Good Friday

The world's pain is preordained
preached Sister Catherine
predictable as one of her sermons
on the importance of good
posture.

Each night I imagined the next
day already unfurling
like the flag of a country
I had sworn allegiance to
my suffering laid out
like the clothes
my mother made me wear.

There was no talking
on Good Friday
between the hours
of noon and three
the hours of the crucifixion
Jesus was put on earth for

though at five minutes past
Mary Lou McGrath whose lips
even in seventh grade seemed other-
worldly wondered in a whisper why
it couldn't have been quicker
the way her cat Shadow just fell
asleep on the stainless steel table.

Mary Lou. Who ended up
marrying a guy who left her
with four kids and another
on the way. Who swore
she never saw it coming.

The Great Molasses Flood
Boston, 1919

From Purity Distilling
down Commercial Street
Atlantic Ave

then on to the harbor
twenty feet high
browning the water

all through that spring
and summer. Hot August
nights the North End still reeks

of it. How absurd
they must think it—
Maria Di Stasio
James Kenneally
all the other dead

drowned
late winter
by so tenacious
a sweetness.

On Edward Hopper's
Rooms by the Sea, 1951

He's left
the damn door open again
and if we'd bought the house
in Hackensack I liked so much
we could stroll out safely
onto tree-lined streets
instead of plummeting into
this misplaced sea.
And what's wrong
with a bit of comfort
in this life?
The place looks barely
lived in
only a glimpse
of our leatherette sofa
the framed watercolor
of Niagara Falls
the green carpet
we bought with the money
my mother left.
Why draw the eye
to the trapezoid
of sunlight along
that horrid wall
we never got around
to decorating
the gaping door
in which the sky hangs
like the dull blade
of a guillotine
and beyond it
all that salt
and stillness?

Malaprops

For all intensive purposes

she's happy
in her colloquial life
never learning to drive
avoiding buses and planes
on account

of her close-aphobia.

How easy it is
to say exactly
what we do not mean.

When I call from far away
she chats
about the garden
the weather
old acquaintances
who've come down

with old-timer's disease.

I never correct her.
Even when she complains
about my taciturn father

and his terrible prostrate troubles.

The Parrot

The tenant next door
doesn't own
a dog or cat
or even a guinea pig
but a teal
and canary-yellow parrot
named Mango.
Blue-fronted Amazons
can live for eighty years
he tells me hopefully.
They're quite intelligent
and require lots
of stimulation.
He can't fly
but hops about ok.
Evenings I see them
sitting on the balcony
like an old couple
content
with just the occasional
word passing
between them.

Breen's Funeral Parlor

My aunts and uncles all ended
up there.

My parents
eventually. But before that

Mr. Breen himself
would visit our shop

most days after school let out
to buy the *Tribune*

and a bottle of Coke.
I'd watch his hands

hairless   thin-veined
nails meticulously trimmed

as they took out his billfold
placed his money on the counter.

I tried to imagine
all that they touched.

They shook slightly as if whispering
something no one wanted

to hear. My father gave him back
his change as though laying bacon

onto a hot skillet.

Ritual

Every Thursday I order ginger ale
and chicken parmesan

my father   the baked haddock.

Even when there's a booth available
he chooses the counter

close to the heat and hiss of the grill

the cook in his pointed paper hat
and bloodied apron

working the dinner rush
like a patrol boat captain

while I, the rear gunner
swivel on my red vinyl stool
between mouthfuls
returning fire.

My father's finally free—

swapping stories
with Jimmy Doucette's dad
and the other regulars

opining about Kennedy
or Conigliaro
unleashing

his startling laugh
engaged in what even now

I understand to be
the great commerce
of men.

Vandals

I always drove. Driving
was the hardest.

You had to concentrate.
Get close enough

with just enough
speed that someone from the back

could lean a little
out the window   lob

a heavy-enough stone to send
the letterbox catapulting

down the road after us.
We loved the precision of it.

It was something to do
on Saturday nights.

We were good kids
wanting to be dangerous

flirting with ruin. Wanting
just to hear the almighty

clatter
of our passing.

Mr. Dombrinski

When we threw a ball accidentally
into his yard we considered it
small loss.

Everyone has places
they dare not go.

We told stories of how he ate
the corpses of neighborhood
kids foolish or slow
enough to get caught.

We dared each other
to egg his house on Halloween
to shaving cream his car.

His blinds were always closed
even in summer.

The few times we heard him call
to his wife or daughter sweeping the drive
or gathering clothes from the line
his voice was harsh and foreign.

We called him *the Nazi*
scribbled it on his fence
once   even after
Billy Pollard's mother told us he'd survived
a camp in Poland.

We'd always find the ball
next morning back
on our side
of the fence.

Fieldstone Wall

Glacial
buried beneath
generations of decay

they mark
the margins
of this field

exhumed
and fitted
one atop another

prominence
to
hollow

held together
by heft
instead of mortar.

Mother
I often wished for you
a tenderness

that could break
you open like the geode
we once unearthed

revealing
all the bright
and jagged crystals.

Commitment

White hair
frames her face
riddled
with effort.

The blue sea
of her hospital gown

spattered
with egg and oatmeal
archipelagoes.

It's 1964
        (it's not)

I'm her husband
        (I'm not)

come
to take her home again
        (never again).

She's lived
in that house for more
than a lifetime, she says. Planted
all the roses.

Her mind is a boat
listing badly—

I consign her
to the sea.

One Hundred and Two

The traffic's barely moving

on the main road out

of my heart.

That's how they explained it.

They said they could fix it

but I told them to save

their gadgets for someone

who could use them.

My memory's good

enough but I'm growing more regretful

every day.

Whoever said practice makes perfect

must have been a young man.

Sit here too long

and you can feel the world

shaking you

off its back like a wet dog.

They tell me I've got cataracts too.

That's why there are clouds

everywhere I look.

Murmurations

Why   they

      sometimes   lift

      at dusk

from their winter   roosts

coalescing
      from   trickle

      to twisting   tide

how they wheel

as one
cohesive cloud
    one being

    is something   known
    or not known
    only to starlings

while we can only watch
from our   distances

    like banished
children   peeking
from bedrooms

while the inscrutable
lives of grown-ups
bank and dive

in other
brightly lit rooms.

Kingfisher

The low angle
of this midwinter sun
casts each blade

of grass in sharp relief
each pebble
in the winding path.

I see you
out of the corner of my eye

not *you* exactly

but a flash of teal
dipping   rising
to its shadowed perch

a thing best seen
like the dimmest of stars
by looking slightly away.

The Evolution of Wings

Fin begot
limb

begot
flight:

the bat's wing
articulate

as small
hands

the slender
scimitars of the albatross

the hummingbird's
hovering

in figures-of-eight
eighty times per second

fixed-wing bombers
striking out from their roosts.

And then
these crickets tonight

whose wings desire
not so much

to fly
as to sing.

Ennui

Cicadas vie
with the neighbor's lawnmower.

Pollen
congealed bird shit

the residue
of rain after rain.

It's more than time
I washed the windows

but today like every day
so much effort

that will only need
repeating.

And anyway when clean
the sparrows fly straight

into them. How
like a fist

the invisible can be.

III

Even this late it happens:
the coming of love, the coming of light
— MARK STRAND

To My Cat Asleep Across the Keyboard

Though you profess
indifference
to poetry

O cat

you are pure
patience
poise
precision

just this
morning

the perfect
metaphor
for *mouse*
left devotedly
by the door.

Ars Poetica #37

Some days
I'm a satellite dish
in a Midwestern front yard
pulling in
a hundred and sixty
stations
including HBO
and The Metaphor Channel.

Some days
I'm a beat
reporter for *The Daily*
the sky wanting to clear
the air
suddenly spill
its side
of the story.

Some days
the blind cat
of my old neighborhood
sitting on our porch
ears twitching
to all the tales
the evening can tell.

Ars Poetica #78

This errant sugar ant

        lured astray

by a false promise

           of sweetness

scuttles   along

the walls

of this fledgling poem

a fleck of frenzied
punctuation

           probing

    each line
for a way out

(or a way in—)

altering   meaning
and meter   with each

sudden
    veer.

How a thing so small
can possess such singleness
of purpose:

to escape

    the glaring
    confines of the page

to find

its pheremonal way

home.

You Say My Poems
Have Too Many Adjectives

As if a lamp
could be just a lamp

a shoe just a way
to get around

as if our lives
didn't need

a bit
of embellishment

could stand
on their own

and be still
worthy of regard.

And you're not
here to see

those mornings
when the traffic lights

the trees
the darkness itself

all wait outside my window
for some small praise.

Crosswords

I'm hunting
for a bird
containing Z
whose feathers
were once used
as money by the Mayans
whose ending
will lead me
down a river
Caesar once crossed
in northern Italy
while across mountains
beginning with A
lies a city south of Paris
where a famous mustard
is right now being made.
Which Greek god
gave us a word
for sudden
uncontrollable fear?
Though some days
I am a giant
book of maps
others, the fabled king
of Melancholia
I still love you
like a five-lettered clasp
used to hold the hair
back from your face.

Synesthesia

Finally you've a name
for what you always thought
was madness:

Tuesdays tinged
an unflattering beige
the sight of persimmons

in late summer
reducing you reliably
to tears

this inescapable feeling
you've smelled
the exact red of her dress

before
the sunlight pooling
in the hollow

above her collarbone
so achingly
you must cover your ears.

Ode to a Platypus

Duck-billed
beaver-bodied
with the legs of a lizard

chimerical—
some might say
comical

though aren't we all
Frankensteins
freakish composites

of that one's nearsightedness
another's large feet
still another's love
of Puccini?

Your hands are not
your own having once belonged
to a man who could never let go
of anything

and the sound of a woman's
footsteps has permanently
replaced your spleen.

We're all outcasts:
half-webbed
half-clawed curiosities—

come swim with me
and we will dive
like mermaids

graceful
as myth.

Man Has Arm Reattached After Shark Attack

—newspaper headline

Synapses
rebuilt
like bombed-out

bridges
touch marching
down dimly remembered

streets like a hometown
hero back
from some distant war

the houses
the storefronts
irrevocably altered

his own body now
like a pointillist painting
viewed at close range

each brushstroke distinct
a hand apart
from what it holds to.

Our War Correspondent Files This Report from Dusk

Honeyed light
strafes the rooftops

between gunships
of low-flying cloud.

Shadows deploy
by open windows

awaiting further orders
grenades of wind

at the ready
weapons loaded

with the hollow
pointed rounds

of birdsong.
In the eastern sky

the mortar shell
of moon

explodes
as night prepares

to drop
its cluster bomb

of stars.

Survival Guide

There's not a menacing cloud
in sight as I sit with this how-to book
remembering a friend

who carried in his briefcase
a pouch of cotton tinder
and waterproof matches
knew which insects are edible

how to gather water
from the transpiration of plants.
He knew to drop and roll if on fire
the safest places to ride

out a tornado
though when his wife of twenty years
left him one ordinary evening
a cyclone of grief caught him

unaware. Survival he said
is a matter of preparation.
And sometimes as in quicksand
not struggling
despite what your instincts scream

the way when attacked by a grizzly
one should play dead and curl inward
to shield the most vulnerable organs.

Man Crushed by 6000 Pound Boulder in Own Backyard

—newspaper headline

And his wife struggling
to fill in

Cause of Death
on the life insurance form.

What can she say except
she told him so?

*There's no end
of ways to go*

she'd warned him
the stubborn fool

trying still
to dig it out

instead of building
the house around it

or even on top it
as she preferred

fancying the notion
of a house teetering

on top of a boulder
all the neighbors amazed

and envious lying
with her husband

in the early mornings to the sound
of the imagined wind

in the improbable
rafters.

Nocturne #47

There are the familiar
noises of nighttime
the house settling
the refrigerator flicking on
the sounds already catalogued

in our subconscious
easy to ignore
as the tedium rasping
behind our lives like crickets.

How quickly fear can travel
the length of our bodies
nerves bristling to attention
         a crash
startling us awake—

we lie huddled in our bed
listening hard
and when nothing follows
we patter hesitantly downstairs
where we find a fallen photograph
of us in our twenties

in a place we've since forgotten
glass shattered   frame splintered
and we are relieved   happy
to sweep up the mess happy
to survive

into another morning
to let the night
have its occasional rant.

Ophidiophobia

Every fear
has its proper

name
in the heart's

vocabulary.
This morning

I disturbed
one

basking beside
the garden wall

a thick
silvered

question mark
I answered

blindly
with the garden spade

every darkness
with its proper

reason.

Arachnophobia

I loved you
for the bold
and merciful way

you would repatriate
stray insects
shooing them back

through open windows
or laying them like
wreaths on the stone

path by the door
but alone now
this spider presents

a paralyzing predicament:
every day's a choice
of what to sacrifice

you said before you left
and so being neither brave
enough nor reverent

I roll today's news
filled with the usual
conflicts

and choose.

Walking the Dog

Past the chihuahua
in its plaid plastic raincoat

the greyhound stepping
like a catwalk model
in stiletto heels

the golden retriever
who reminds me vaguely
of Jimmy O'Loughlin
a decent guy I knew

in high school who married
Judy Robillard when he got her
pregnant

was mad about sports
and asked me every lunchtime
You gonna finish that sandwich?

Like old couples they say
dogs and owners come to
resemble one another

and today I see myself clearly

in your cocoa eyes
disappointed but conditioned
to please

as I call you back
from the underbrush

where you chased a rabbit
you'd no hope
of catching.

Damn Right I Let the Cat Out

because we all have to fend
for ourselves eventually.

And yes, I ate the last of the chocolates
which once I might have saved for you.

Today I did fifty above the speed limit.
Broke the code of silence

dropped *shit* and *fuck* gratuitously
into the very same poem

like tattooed gangbangers
into our leafy suburbia.

Didn't you ever want to graffiti up
the wall of your existence

for no good reason?

Because it's clear you'll never leap
the Grand Canyon on a star-spangled rocket bike?

Because you you'll never be the Big Kahuna?
Never land the Big One?

Because you're not the rock-star
strutting onstage in studded boots

some days not even the middle-aged usher
who gets to watch

after showing John Q. Public
to his goddamned seat?

Turbulence

Descending
        toward a city constructed

on faulty lines

            a city of blind
faith
     in the beneficent

we enter a bank
of clouds

           and for a time fly
     on instruments
and instinct

our own blindness
our own

faith   buffeted

by rogue winds

(*I should have left out extra cat food.*

Who'll buy you that expensive coffee you love?)

still far
     from the coastline

we're turning for

where bright houses cling desperately
to the steep

          sides
of hills.

Benedictions

When the telephone startles
you awake at four in the morning

may it be just a friend
from another time zone.

When the truck swerves over
the yellow line

may you be running late
having dawdled over eggs

over-easy. When you meet an old love
at the market may you be tanned

from a month by the sea.
May you rise even once

from your foreseeable life
in some foreign country

the sun blinding
off the brackish waters

of a river whose name
you cannot pronounce.

And if you settle finally
along a deep fault

line may it be with someone
who holds you each night

as though you were bone
china and the whole house were trembling.

The Day the Music Died

Sometimes
even death can't bear
another bus ride
between cold Midwestern towns
clothes that reek
of smoke and sweat.

Sometimes
death just wins
the coin toss
comes down with the flu
and wants
to get to bed early.

Sometimes
death just wants
to hear its song
sung over
and over
on the radio.

Black Swans

after Karl Popper

To find the truth
look for black swans.

These two come
every fall

though I'm not sure
they're the same pair—

there are so many
truths

that look alike.
I've heard they mate

for life
and today I just need

it to be true
even if it isn't

for the sake
of this poem

and every poem.

The Green and Golden Bell Frog

In a baritone
like old men laughing

at the best damn joke
they've heard in years

these amorous wetland frogs
bellow

their vitality
through the open window

keeping me awake
with their cacophony

while you sleep
undisturbed

except
for the occasional   twitch

of your leg entwined
with mine

the rhythmic thrall
of your breathing

a lesson they could learn
in love's quiet insistence.

Guilty

Every choice I make
spells demise.
Every word wounds.
Every breath perturbs
the atmospheric balance
raises the oceans by degrees.

Today I was going to change
but again stumbled through
my life tipping the balance
against some fragile thing
waffling on the edge of extinction.

Perhaps I should shave my head
wrap myself in monk's saffron
although the cloth of my conviction
will likely have been woven
in some sweatshop
by a child subsisting on my desire
for salvation.

Perhaps I should lock
myself away
like a recalcitrant criminal.
It's all I can do some nights
to hold my breath
lay my head on the goose-down pillow
and wait for you to wake
my sweet accessory-after-the-fact.

ACKNOWLEDGEMENTS

Thanks to the editors of the following magazines where these poems or previous versions of them first appeared:

East Coast Literary Review: Ode to a Platypus

Front Porch Review: You Say My Poems Have Too Many Adjectives, The Day the Music Died

Harvard Review: Man Has Arm Reattached After Shark Attack

Innisfree Poetry Journal: Fieldstone Wall, Ophidiophobia

The Kentucky Review: Magician Dreams, Ennui

Salamander: Crosswords

San Pedro River Review: Heroes

Our War Correspondent Files This Report from Dusk was published in *Poems4Peace Anthology* by Printable Reality Press, NZ, 2014

Inchoate was published in Fresh Ink, A Collection of Voices from Aoteroa New Zealand, Cloud Ink Press, 2017

Multitudes, Commitment, and One Hundred and Two were first published online via The Medicine Stories Project (themedicinestoriesproject.co.nz)

I'd like to offer heart-felt thanks to all those long-suffering friends and family who have indulged my reckless love of poetry, especially Rhonda, Evan, Cameron, Stu Bagby and the members of my Tuesday writers group who have assisted in the editing of many of these poems.

www.ingramcontent.com/pod-product-compliance
Lightning Source LLC
Chambersburg PA
CBHW050918160426
43194CB00011B/2460